CLEAN & UNCLEAN

Activity Book for Beginners

Clean & Unclean Activity Book for Beginners

Bible Pathway Adventures® is a trademark of BPA Publishing Ltd.
Defenders of the Faith® is a trademark of BPA Publishing Ltd.

ISBN: 978-1-98-858539-0

Author: Pip Reid
Creative Director: Curtis Reid

For free Bible resources including coloring pages, worksheets, puzzles and more, visit our website at:

www.biblepathwayadventures.com

 # Introduction for Parents

Your children will LOVE learning about clean and unclean animals of the Bible with this hands-on Clean and Unclean Activity Book for Beginners. Each page invites them to learn about clean and unclean animals, birds, and marine animals through coloring, tracing, and writing activities. Designed to help you teach your children the basics of clean and unclean animals (Deuteronomy 14 and Leviticus 11) in a fun and creative way. The perfect discipleship resource for Homeschoolers, Sabbath and Sunday School teachers, and parents.

Bible Pathway Adventures helps educators and parents teach children about the Biblical faith in a fun creative way. We do this via our illustrated storybooks, Activity Books, and printable activities – available for download on our website www.biblepathwayadventures.com

Thanks for buying this Activity Book and supporting our ministry. Every book purchased helps us continue our work providing Classroom Packs and discipleship resources to families and missions around the world.

The search for Truth is more fun than Tradition!

 # Table of Contents

Coloring pages

Flashcards:

Crafts & Projects

This book belongs to:

....

Draw something

My favorite animal

Clean and Unclean

Read Leviticus 11 and Deuteronomy 14.
Common clean and unclean animals, birds, and marine animals include:

Clean:

Antelope

Buffalo

Cows and sheep

Deer

Dove

Duck

Giraffe

Goat

Moose

Peacock

Quail

Sparrow (plus any other songbirds)

Turkey and chicken

Clean insects include types of locusts that may include crickets and grasshoppers.

Fish with scales

Unclean:

Bear

Camel

Cats & Dogs

Crocodile

Donkey

Elephant

Frog

Hippopotamus

Horse

Lion

Monkey

Mouse

Pig

Rabbit

Snake

Wolf

Worm

Zebra

All insects except some in the locust family.

Crab, crayfish, and lobsters

Prawn, shrimp, mussels, oysters, and scallops

Sharks and dolphins

✶ I am clean! ✶

Trace the words. Color the picture.

I am a cow

Can you eat me?

I am clean!

Trace the words. Color the picture.

I am a sheep

Can you eat me?

I am clean!

Trace the words. Color the picture.

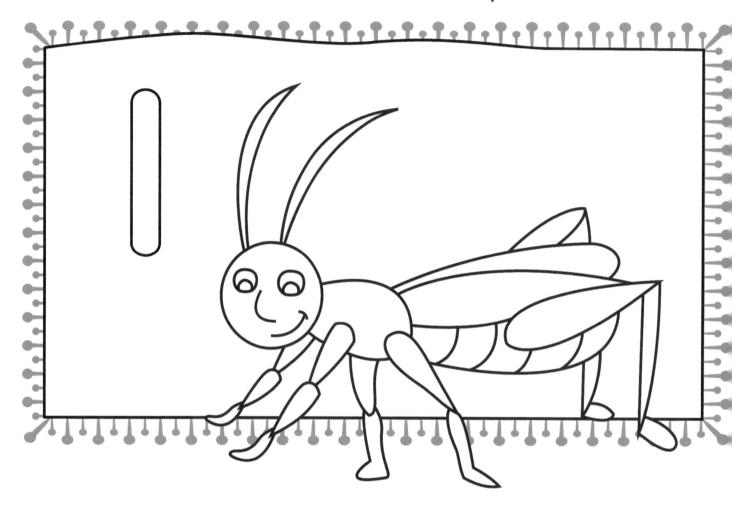

I am a locust

Can you eat me?

I am clean!

Trace the words. Color the picture.

I am a deer

Can you eat me?

I am clean!

Trace the words. Color the picture.

I am a goat

Can you eat me?

I am clean!

Trace the words. Color the picture.

I am a fish with scales

Can you eat me?

I am clean!

Trace the words. Color the picture.

I am a moose

Can you eat me?

Bible Pathway
— Adventures —

I am clean!

Trace the words. Color the picture.

I am a chicken

Can you eat me?

I am clean!

Trace the words. Color the picture.

I am a buffalo

Can you eat me?

I am clean!

Trace the words. Color the picture.

I am a turkey

Can you eat me?

I am clean!

Trace the words. Color the picture.

I am an antelope

Can you eat me?

I am clean!

Trace the words. Color the picture.

g

I am a giraffe

Can you eat me?

I am clean!

Trace the words. Color the picture.

I am a duck

Can you eat me?

✶ I am clean! ✶

Trace the words. Color the picture.

I am a peacock

Can you eat me?

✦ I am Unclean! ✦

Trace the words. Color the picture.

d

I am a donkey

Can you eat me?

I am Unclean!

Trace the words. Color the picture.

I am a pig

Can you eat me?

I am Unclean!

Trace the words. Color the picture.

I am a lion

Can you eat me?

I am Unclean!

Trace the words. Color the picture.

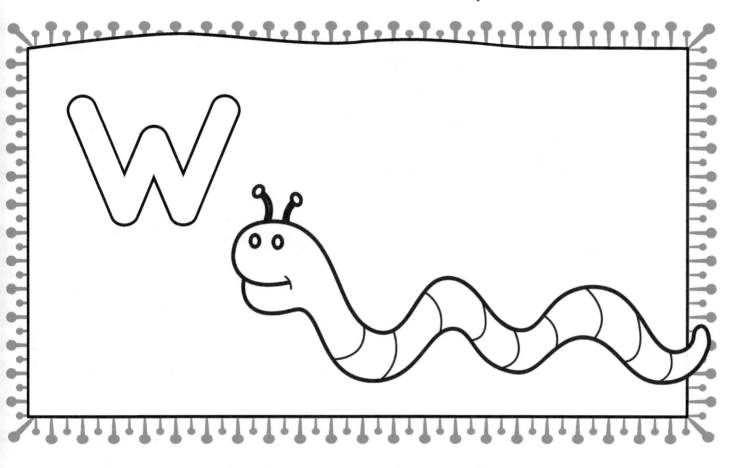

I am a worm

Can you eat me?

I am Unclean!

Trace the words. Color the picture.

I am a camel

Can you eat me?

I am Unclean!

Trace the words. Color the picture.

f

I am a frog

Can you eat me?

I am Unclean!

Trace the words. Color the picture.

h

I am a hippo

Can you eat me?

I am Unclean!

Trace the words. Color the picture.

I am a snake

Can you eat me?

I am Unclean!

Trace the words. Color the picture.

I am a dog

Can you eat me?

I am Unclean!

Trace the words. Color the picture.

I am a monkey

Can you eat me?

I am Unclean!

Trace the words. Color the picture.

I am a rabbit

Can you eat me?

I am Unclean!

Trace the words. Color the picture.

I am a crab

Can you eat me?

I am Unclean!

Trace the words. Color the picture.

S

I am a shrimp

Can you eat me?

I am Unclean!

Trace the words. Color the picture.

I am an elephant

Can you eat me?

Clean and unclean animals

Count and color the clean animals.
Write an "X" on the unclean animals.

🌿 Clean animals 🌿

Find and circle each of the words from the list below.

```
C  D  K  P  M  G
O  E  N  K  O  O
W  E  A  W  O  A
N  R  V  D  S  T
F  I  S  H  E  E
S  H  E  E  P  Y
```

SHEEP	COW
MOOSE	DEER
FISH	GOAT

Unclean animals

Find and circle each of the words from the list below.

```
L F S A D S
I R L C O H
O O N D N R
N G N O K I
M D O G E M
P I G F Y P
```

LION   DOG

DONKEY   SHRIMP

PIG   FROG

Clean and unclean animals

Trace the names. Color the animals.

goat

fish

moose

chicken

buffalo

turkey

antelope

giraffe

duck

peacock

donkey

pig

	lion
	worm
	camel
	frog

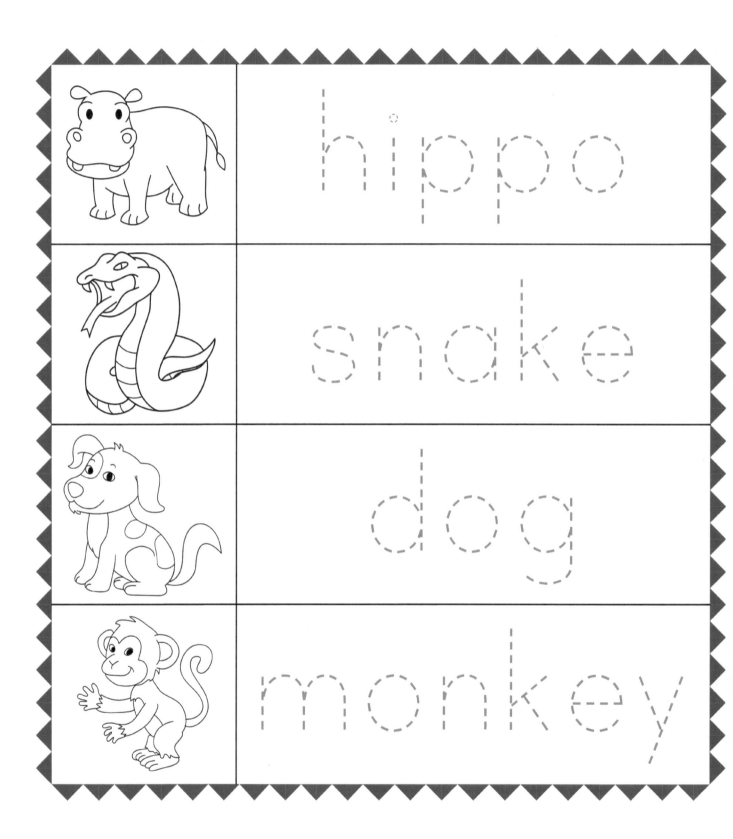

hippo

snake

dog

monkey

rabbit

crab

shrimp

elephant

Clean and unclean animals

How many clean and unclean animals & insects do you know?
Write the correct name below each picture. Color the picture

- -

- -

- -

- - - - - - - - - -

Clean and unclean animals

Write the names of the clean and unclean animals in the correct column.

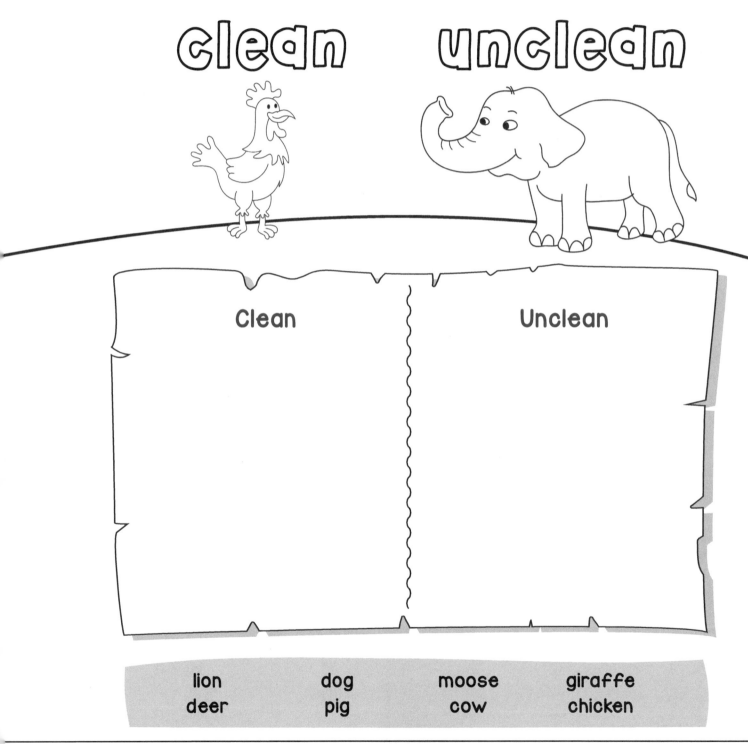

clean   unclean

Clean	Unclean

lion	dog	moose	giraffe
deer	pig	cow	chicken

Flashcards

🌿 Flashcards 🌿

Color and cut out the flashcards.
Hang them around your home or classroom!

cow

1

sheep

2

locust

3

deer

4

goat

5

fish

6

moose

7

chicken

8

buffalo

9

turkey

10

antelope

11

giraffe

12

duck

13

peacock

14

donkey

15

pig

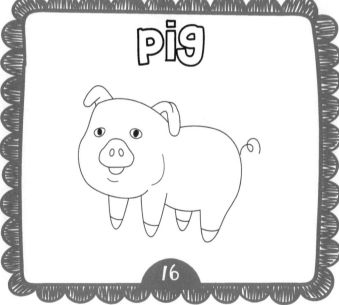

16

lion

17

worm

18

camel

19

frog

20

hippo

21

snake

22

dog

23

monkey

24

rabbit

25

crab

26

Shrimp

27

elephant

28

Crafts & Projects

Place the animals on the ark

On Noah's ark, there were seven pairs of every
clean animal and two pairs of every unclean animal.
Cut out the animals and place them on the ark.
Which animals are clean? Which are unclean?

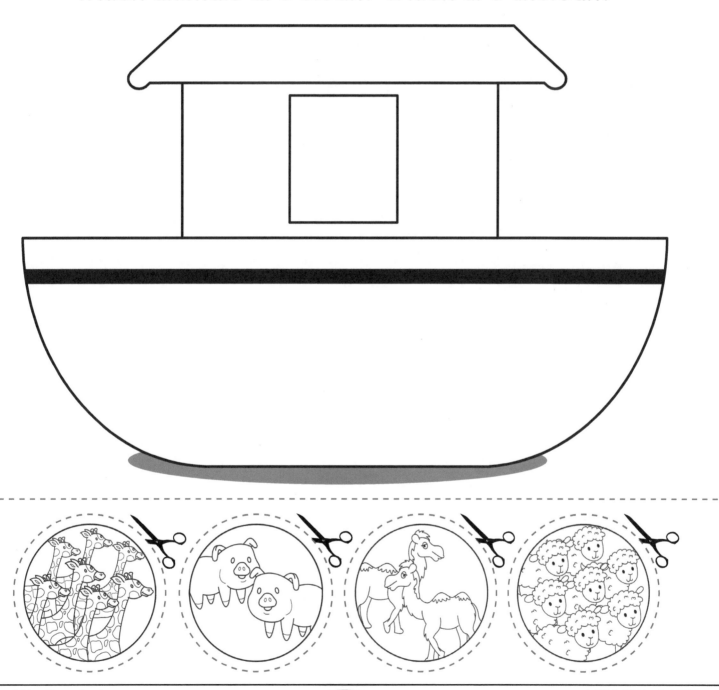

Discover more Activity Books!

Available for purchase at www.biblepathwayadventures.com

INSTANT DOWNLOAD!

The Spring Feasts
The Spring Feasts (Beginners)
The Fall Feasts (Beginners)
Learning Hebrew: The Alphabet
Learning Hebrew: Clothes
Learning Hebrew: Let's Eat!
Learning Hebrew: Fruit & Vegetables

Twelve Tribes of Israel (Beginners)